THE 30-MINUTE PLANT-BASED COOKBOOK FOR BEGINNERS

QUICK AND EASY VEGETARIAN COOKBOOK FOR BEGINNERS. START YOUR JOURNEY IN VEGETARIANISM WITH 30-MINUTES DELICIOUS RECIPES. 10 NEW RECIPES INCLUDED

Shioban Cruw

TABLE OF CONTENTS

Introduction   **9**

Chapter 1: Introduction to vegetarian.   **11**

Benefits of a Vegetarian Diet   *15*

Foods To Eat And Foods To Avoid   *16*

Vegetarian Sources of Vitamins and Protein   *19*

Chapter 2: Breakfast   **21**

Breakfast Egg Sandwich   *21*

Cottage Cheese Griddlecakes   *23*

Amaranth Oat Waffles   *25*

Blueberry Baked Oatmeal   *27*

French Toast with Strawberries   *29*

Dark and Addictive Bran Muffins   *31*

Brown Rice Breakfast   *33*

Smoothie on the Beach   *35*

Buttermilk Bran Pancakes   *37*

Mexican Tomatillo-Poblano Eggs   *39*

Vegetable Cheese Strata   *41*

Creamy Fruit-Filled Crepes   *43*

Breakfast Tacos   *45*

Rice and Bean Frittata   *47*

Breakfast Pita Pizzas   *49*

Waffle Sandwiches   *51*

Peanut Butter and Fruit Quinoa   *53*

Easy Huevos Rancheros   *55*

Oat Flour Pancakes   57

Chapter 3: Salads and dressings   59

Artichoke and Green Olives with Walnut Vinaigrette   59

Swiss Chard and Artichoke Hearts with Black Olive Salad   61

Collard Greens Black Olive and Artichoke Heart Salad   63

Heart with Macadamia Vinaigrette Salad   65

Bib Lettuce Black Olives and Artichoke Heart Salad   67

Boston Lettuce with Black Olive Salad   69

Romaine Lettuce with Artichoke Heart and Cashew Vinaigrette Salad   71

Mustard Greens Artichoke Heart and Green Olive Salad   73

Beetroot Kalamata Olives and Artichoke Heart Salad   75

Collard Greens Baby Corn and Artichoke Heart Salad   77

Boston Lettuce Baby Carrots and Artichoke Heart Salad   79

Kale Black Olives and Baby Corn Salad   81

Romaine Lettuce & Baby Carrots with Walnut Vinaigrette Salad   83

Boston Lettuce with Capers and Artichoke Heart Salad   85

Bib Lettuce Olive and Baby Carrot with Walnut Vinaigrette Salad   86

Collard Greens with Baby Corn Salad   87

Boston Lettuce Red Onion and Artichoke Heart with Peanut Vinaigrette Salad   88

Bib Lettuce Black Olives and Baby Corn with Almond Vinaigrette Salad   89

Endive and Green Olive Salad   90

Mixed Greens Olives and Artichoke Heart Salad   91

Iceberg Lettuce and Artichoke Heart Salad   92

Artichoke Capers and Artichoke Heart Salad   93

Mixed Greens Baby Corn and Artichoke Heart Salad   94

Bib Lettuce with Tomatillo Dressing   95

Enoki Mushroom and Cucumber Salad   96

Tomato and Zucchini Salad   97

Plum Tomato and Onion Salad   99

Zucchini Pepperjack Cheese and Tomato Salad   100

Heirloom Tomato Salad   101

Enoki Mushroom and Feta Cheese Salad   102

Artichoke Heart and Plum Tomato Salad   103

Artichoke Heart and Plum Tomato Salad   104

Baby Corn and Plum Tomato Salad   106

Mixed Greens Feta Cheese and Tomato Salad   108

Artichoke and Tomato Salad   110

Spinach and Heirloom Tomato Salad   111

Mesclun and Tomatillo Salad   113

Mesclun and Enoki Mushroom Salad   115

Bib Lettuce and Cucumber Salad   117

Kale Spinach and Zucchini with Cream Cheese Salad   119

Artichoke Spinach and Enoki Mushroom Salad   120

Kale and Artichoke Salad   121

Conclusion   **122**

Introduction

Vegetarianism refers to a lifestyle that excludes the consumption of all forms of meat including pork, chicken, beef, lamb, venison, fish, and shells. Depending on a person belief and lifestyle, vegetarianism has different spectrums. There are vegetarians, who like to consume products that come from animals such as milk, eggs, cream and cheese. On the other end of that spectrum are the vegans. Vegans never consume meat or any product that comes from animals.

I firmly believe every decision we make in life, regardless of how well-calculated the move is, has good and bad consequences. Your dietary habit is no exception; in fact, your food choices significantly impact overall health and wellbeing. Precisely, when it comes to dieting, the rule of thumb here is simple; proper nutrition results in healthy living and satisfaction.

However, we live in a world where new dietary habits crop up every day. Besides, today, people are redefining the old dietary practices to suit the modern lifestyle. New dietary habits, coupled with the complexity of today's lifestyle, put the world on a collision course with the principles of healthy living. What encourages me, however, is the fact that some dietary practices like vegetarianism have stood the test of time.

However, if you have decided to go vegetarian life, congratulations, you have made a brilliant decision. This because commitment to vegetarianism is a dedication to good health. And luckily for you, I have written this book to hold your hand during the transition. The book will see you through the journey, opening up horizons of whole new meals that you will adore.

Regardless of your reason for going vegetarian, you will adore this cookbook. Whether it is for religious or health purposes, I have unpacked the information you need and served it up in a way that is easy to understand. Besides, I will give you cooking tips that will help you nail vegetarianism and make it part of your lifestyle. Trust me, the journey will be bumpy, but with this cookbook, you have a partner to keep you going even when things seem to be grinding to a halt.

As if that is not enough, this book has simple recipes to get you started. Everything from salads, appetizers, and mains, each Directions is designed to complement your health and those crazy cravings. I went for recipes with five ingredients or less, to give you a smooth ride in the kitchen.

Trust me, with this cookbook; you will love vegetables even before you know it. This cookbook is not only the best vegetarian book with tons of recipes but also a simple guide to vegetarianism and benefits to it. If looking forward to vegetarianism for the rest of your life, this cookbook is for you.

Chapter 1: Introduction to vegetarian.

Vegetarian diets are most often much lower in sugars and fat than a meat based diet; though just cutting meat out is no guarantee of weight loss. Vegetarians are still tempted by junk food, highly processed foods and other unhealthy foods too. If you are planning on losing weight by becoming a vegetarian then you need to follow some other basic weight loss strategies to ensure you lose the weight you want.

One of the main benefits to you of the vegetarian diet is that it is lower in saturated fat (though be wary of convenience vegetarian foods which are high in these unhealthy fats) and has a higher intake of fresh fruit and vegetables. This makes a vegetarian leaner than a meat eater, so long as they are not a junk food addict.

Being a vegan means even less saturated fat as you do not eat dairy or eggs, so technically you can lose more weight. However, it is down to your personal preference, your lifestyle and your tastes. Going vegan for a few weeks can help kick start your weight loss.

Just stopping eating meat isn't going to help you lose weight if you are still consuming huge amounts of calories every day. You will need to discipline yourself and control your calorie intake like you would on any diet. However, remember that vegetables in particular are low in calories and most diets instruct you to "pile 'em high" on your plate!

Just watch your portion sizes, particularly with the more fattening foods that you eat; the same goes for restaurants. Prepare your meals in advance and plan what you are going to eat and you will find it much easier to lose weight. Also make sure you have some healthy, low fat snacks around so you are less likely to reach for a candy bar.

Try to avoid frying food when you can and bake, steam or grill instead because it is lower in fat and much healthier for you.

In order to lose weight reliably you will need to increase your exercise levels to burn fat and excess calories. Regular cardio and weight training will help to improve your health and help you process food better. You can lose some weight as a vegetarian but to really turbo-charge your weight loss you need to incorporate exercise into your daily regime. Join a gym, get a personal trainer and start working out because you will find your weight loss speeds up and that you lose inches as you start to firm up your muscles.

The main component of your diet will be vegetables and fruits, together with beans and whole grains. With all meats and fish eliminated from your diet you are already eating many of the foods that are recommended by diet plans to help you lose weight. Studies have shown that a low fat vegan diet alone will help you to lose 1lb a week without including exercise or any other factors!

Be aware though that if you are loading up on pasta, cereal and breads (high carbohydrate / low nutrition) then you will struggle to lose weight. Eating too many sugary foods or the meat substitutes is also going to contribute to you not losing weight. Remember that by applying these principles to your vegetarian diet you will speed up your weight loss and improve your health further.

A vegan will eliminate all meat products from their diet including eggs, dairy and gelatine. Typically a vegan will avoid any products that are made from animals such as leather, wool, down, silk and so on. Many vegans choose to follow this lifestyle because they have care deeply for animals and the environment.

Vegetarians however will wear leather, wool and silk and many will eat eggs and dairy products. Most vegetarians will avoid products that contain gelatine though some will quietly ignore it as it is in such a tiny quantity. It is your choice which you follow at the end of the day.

Nutritionally there is not a huge amount of difference between a pure vegetarian and a vegan; the latter will need a vitamin B12 supplement. A lacto-ovo vegetarian should not need this supplement as they will get it from eggs and dairy. For those that choose the vegan approach it is usually related to their love and respect for animals. From a weight loss point of view, a vegan diet can help to kick-start your weight loss and help you lose an extra couple of pounds when you need it.

Whether you start off as a vegetarian and do weeks of vegan eating or what type of vegetarian diet you choose to follow is entirely up to you. Make sure you have thought through all the different options and selected the right type of diet for you.

Whilst the vegetarian diet is going to help you to lose weight, it is also going to help to improve your health. A lot of research has been performed in to the benefits of vegetarianism, and the result is the federal government even recommend that the majority of your daily calories come from vegetables, fruits and grain products.

It is estimated that around 70% of all diseases, including a third of all cancers are caused by diet! Vegetarians have a lower risk of obesity, high blood pressure, diabetes, coronary artery disease and cancers including prostate, stomach, breast, oesophageal and colon cancer. You can already see the benefits of cutting out meat!

You will be interested in knowing that vegetarians are typically healthier than the average American, particularly when it comes to reversing heart disease and reducing the risks of cancers. A low fat vegetarian diet has been proven to be the best way to stop coronary artery disease progressing or to prevent it.

Every year, over a million people in American die from cardiovascular disease; it's the number one killer in the USA. However, the mortality rate from this disease is significantly lower in vegetarians due to the lower cholesterol levels and that you consume less saturated fat. A vegetarian will consume more anti-oxidants, more fiber and more vitamins and minerals.

The standard Western diet is high in processed foods full of chemicals, sugar and salt and low in plant based foods. This diet is actually killing us all slower. The obesity statistics are shocking and the associated health problems even worse.

Between the years of 1986 and 1992 the Preventive Medicine Research Institute in Sausalito California conducted a study in to the vegetarian diet. They discovered that an overweight person who ate a low fat vegetarian diet lost, on average, twenty four pounds in year one and in five year's time had still kept the weight off. This weight was lost without feeling hungry, measuring portions or counting calories.

Studies have also shown that a vegetarian diet will extend your life by around thirteen years of good health! Meat eaters will typically not only have a shorter lifespan but will also suffer from more disabilities at the end of their lives. Studies have also shown that meat eaters also experience sexual and cognitive dysfunction at a younger age.

A fringe benefit of vegetarianism is that your risk of food borne illness is dramatically reduced. According to CDC statistics there are 76,000,000 food borne illnesses each year across the United States. The majority of these illnesses come from meat and seafood!

The vegetarian diet also eases the symptoms of the menopause, particularly as soy is the best natural source of phytoestrogens, but they are also found in many other vegetables too. As women often gain weight during the menopause as their metabolism slows down, a low fat vegetarian diet can help keep the extra pounds off.

Another advantage of the vegetarian diet is that your energy levels increase. As you are not spending so much of your energy digesting heavy foods. The foods you eat as a vegetarian tend to be more nutritious, meaning your body has the vitamins it needs to be healthy.

A good, balanced vegetarian diet is free from the saturated fats that clog up your arteries and restricts the oxygen supply to your body. Your diet will also be high in complex carbohydrates which give you more energy that lasts longer.

Vegetarians also help the environment with meat production causing deforestation, global warming and more. According to the EPA in the USA, animal and chemical waste runoff from factory farming causes over 173,000 miles of polluted streams and rivers.

Many of the toxins a human eats come from meat and seafood, with fish in particular storing heaving metals and carcinogens that cannot be removed. Many meat and dairy products also have high levels of growth hormones, steroids and antibiotics which are taken in to your body.

Around 70% of the grain produced in the USA is fed to animals. There are around seven billion livestock animals in the United States which consume five times more grain than the American population itself. The grain fed to animals is worth about $80 billion on the export market and would feed around 800 million people!

Every year over ten billion animals are slaughtered for human consumption, which is a major factor for many vegetarians in giving up meat. That and the treatment of animals – factory farming, force feeding, poor conditions and so on. What you may not realize is that state laws on animal cruelty specifically exclude farm animals from even the most basic, humane protection.

Being a vegetarian is cheaper, particular if you don't rely on the expensive textured vegetable protein used as a meat substitute. Around 10% of the average American's income is spent on meat. By cutting out the meat, on average, you could save around $4,000 a year!

The vegetarian's dinner plate is always full of color, which means they are full of vital vitamins and minerals. Yellow and orange foods are high in carotenoids, as are leafy green vegetables, which are also high in chlorophyll. Red and purple foods are high in anthocyanins. These are both important for your health and will help boost your immune system.

With so many personal and environmental benefits to being a vegetarian your plan to lose weight suddenly seems even more appealing. You will notice that as you lose weight you feel healthier, have more energy and are able to enjoy life more because of it.

Benefits of a Vegetarian Diet

Lower risk of stroke and obesity

Vegetarians contribute to be much more having knowledge of their food choices and generally never overeat or choose foods that are based on emotions, two practices that contribute significantly to obesity. The Paediatric Department at the University Hospital of Ghent in Belgium believes that a vegan diet is an excellent way to minimize the risk of stroke or obesity.

Get healthy skin

If you want to have healthy skin, you need to take the right amount of vitamins and minerals with plenty of water. The fruits and vegetables we eat are very rich in vitamins, minerals, and antioxidants. Because they are water-based, they can improve your intake of healthy nutrients when consumed raw. Many vegetarian foods are also rich in antioxidants that allow you to stay disease-free and have more youthful skin.

Reduce depression

According to studies, a vegetarian could be happier than his non-vegetarian counterparts. It was also found that a vegetarian had lower levels of depression and swinging mood profiles compared to the non-vegetarians. Besides, most vegetarian diets contain an element of freshness, especially for organic products, therefore obligated to cleanse our mind and also keep our thoughts positive.

Reduce the risk of cataracts

According to a study by the Oxford University Nuffield Clinical Medicine Department, there is a close correlation between the risk of developing cataracts and our diet, higher risk for non-vegetarians or meat consumers, and a lower risk of being vegan.

Economical

Lastly, you will save a lot of money if you are vegetarian. Without a doubt, non-vegetarian foods are expensive compared to vegetarian foods.

Extend the life

Although many factors are due to an increase in life, it is possible to eat a vegetarian diet. The more fruits or vegetables you eat, the fewer toxins and chemicals you accumulate in your body, leading to healthier years and longer life.

Foods To *Eat* And Foods To Avoid

As a vegetarian you will avoid all meat and seafood products, though some will eat eggs and dairy. On top of this there are a lot of other things that a vegetarian can eat and this section is designed to help you understand how the vegetarian diet works and what foods you can eat and enjoy.

Grains

Grains are an important part of the vegetarian diet and it is recommended that you eat between five and seven servings per day, of which half should be whole grains. Grains include oats, barley, wheat, rice, bread and pasta, many of which are now fortified with vitamins such as zinc, iron and vitamin B-12 which are more commonly found in meat and seafood.

Proteins

Non-vegetarians get their protein from meat, but you will need to get your protein from other sources including beans, legumes, soy and nuts. For those who eat it, dairy and eggs are a good source of protein too. Iron normally comes from meat but instead you can find it in dry beans, lentils, soybeans, tofu, peas and spinach. Remember to consume foods rich in vitamin C at the same time as they help you absorb iron.

Fruits And Vegetables

Fruits and vegetables are consumed in large amounts by a vegetarian. Whether these are fresh or frozen is entirely up to you, but whichever you choose they are high in vitamins and minerals. You want between six and eight servings of vegetables every day and three or four of fruit. If you are not eating eggs or dairy then make sure you eat plenty of dark green leafy vegetables as they are high in nutrients your body needs.

Fats

We are taught that low fat diets are good for us, but your diet needs to be low in saturated fats. The proper fats are important for the operation of your body and you need around two servings per day. You need fats that are high in Omega-3 fatty acids which you can get from an ounce of nuts or seeds, a teaspoon of olive oil or two tablespoons of nut butter.

As a vegetarian you will be eating plenty of nutrient dense foods though because of the lack of meat, particularly if you are avoiding dairy and eggs, you may need to take some supplements to ensure you are getting the right nutrients.

Foods To Be Careful Of

As a vegetarian you will need to be careful about some of the foods you are eating because meat does creep into rather a lot of foods.

This section will help you understand what foods you need to watch out for.

Soups are delicious and great for a vegetarian, but be careful when dining out or buying cans of soup as often they will be made with a chicken, beef or fish base. Make sure you ask in a restaurant and read the ingredients on the can just to be sure, but it is easy to make your own delicious soups at home!

A lot of salad dressings in restaurants are built on bacon fat and Caesar dressing contains anchovies. Make sure you check the ingredients in the dressing to make sure it is vegetarian friendly and doesn't have an animal hiding in it.

Cheese is eaten by some vegetarians but not all cheese is vegetarian! Some cheeses use animal rennet in their manufacturing, which is enzymes from animal stomachs! You will find cheeses that are vegetarian or you can ignore this fact, it is up to you. If you check the labels you will find the vegetarian cheeses are labelled as such.

If you eat tortillas then check the ingredients as many of them are made with animal products, as are many other chips. Some of the meaty flavors of chip are in fact vegetarian and typically they will be labelled so you know what you can and cannot eat.

Look out for gummy type sweets as well as usually these will contain gelatine which comes from animal bones. There are some vegetarian versions if you are being strict, though a lot of vegetarians will overlook this fact in their need for candy! Check the ingredients of Jello and marshmallows as these can also contain gelatine.

And bad news for many men here, some beers aren't entirely vegetarian as they can be clarified with something called isinglass or fish bladders. Some beers are fine, though it is up to you how strict you want to be here.

There are a lot of foods that you may think are safe to eat but are in fact not vegetarian. Take some time to read the labels and you will soon work out which foods you can and cannot eat following the above guidelines.

Vegetarian Sources of Vitamins and Protein

A vegetarian who doesn't eat the right type of diet could end up with chronic fatigue and a compromised immune system, so it is important that you eat the right types of food.

Firstly, you need to decide what type of vegetarian diet you are going to follow. A lacto-ovo vegetarian is going to get a lot of more essential nutrients than a pure vegan, but you can still be healthy when following the latter diet.

You need to understand the vitamin content of food and ensure that you eat a balanced diet that includes plenty of fruit and vegetables, as these are your primary sources of vitamins. You want around six to eight portions of vegetables and three to four of fruit every single day. If you are not getting these then you are going to become deficient in vital nutrients.

Protein is essential and it isn't hard to get the required levels on a vegetarian diet. However, you need to make sure it is coming from good sources such as tofu, beans, lentils, chickpeas and so on. You can get protein from textured vegetable proteins (meat replacements) though this is highly processed and can contain chemicals, saturated fats and other unwanted additives.

You can also get your protein from whole grains and leafy green vegetables as well as dairy products and eggs. If you are concerned about your protein levels, then you can use vegetarian protein powders mixed into smoothies or juices.

If you feel that you are lacking in the proper nutrition, then get some vitamin tablets and start taking them. You may find you are not getting enough vitamin B-12, calcium and iron but you can get iron from mushrooms, tofu and cashew nuts. If you do choose to take an iron supplement then you will need to also take a vitamin C supplement to help you absorb the iron.

Calcium is found in the leafy green vegetables as well as fortified products such as soy milk and so on. If you are taking a calcium supplement, then also take a vitamin D supplement as this will help you absorb the calcium properly.

B-12 is the big problem for pure vegans because it is found in animal products and not in vegetables. However, you can get this from fortified yeasts, cereal or soy milk. It is found in eggs and dairy products if you are a lacto-ovo vegetarian.

You will also need Omega-3 fatty acids which are vital for your brain development, eyesight and muscles. This is found in eggs but can also be found in pure vegetarian sources such as soybeans, tofu, walnuts, flaxseed oil and canola oil. If you are in doubt about how much of this you are getting then take a supplement.

When you are getting the right nutrition from your vegetarian diet you will feel fantastic and really benefit from following this way of eating. Make sure you are getting all the right vitamins and if you feel you aren't then take some supplements to give your system a boost.

Chapter 2: Breakfast

Breakfast Egg Sandwich

Preparation time: 15 minutes
Cooking time: 3 minutes
Servings: 1

 Ingredients

Whole wheat bagel – 1, split

Dijon mustard – 1 tsp.

Yogurt cheese – 2 Tbsp.

Avocado – ¼, slightly mashed

Tomato – 2 to 3 slices

Alfalfa sprouts - ¼ cup

Whole egg – 1 + 2 egg whites

Pinch sea salt and black pepper

Cooking spray

Directions

First, set up oven rack about six inches from the top of oven and turn on broiler.

Toast the bagel under the broiler (cut side up).

Spread both sides of a toasted bagel with Dijon mustard and yogurt cheese. On the top half of the bagel, spread mashed avocado and add the tomato slices and sprouts.

Heat a skillet and spray with cooking spray.

Beat eggs with salt and pepper and pour into the skillet.

Cook until firm.

Arrange the eggs with the bagel and serve.

Cottage Cheese Griddlecakes

Preparation time: 5 minutes
Cooking time: 20 minutes
Servings: 14

Ingredients

Whole wheat flour – 1 ¼ cups

Baking powder – 2 tsp.

Baking soda – ½ tsp.

Unrefined sugar – 3 Tbsp.

Pinch freshly grated nutmeg

Pinch sea salt

Low-fat milk – 1 cup

Low-fat cottage cheese – 1 cup

Egg yolk – 1

Vanilla extract – 1 tsp.

Finely grated lemon zest – 1 tsp.

Egg whites – 3

Cooking spray

Directions

In a bowl, whisk together sugar, nutmeg, baking soda, baking powder, salt, and flour.

In another bowl, whisk together cottage cheese, milk, egg yolk, vanilla extract, and lemon zest.

Mix both wet and dry ingredients until just combined.

Add egg whites to a separate bowl and beat them into stiff peaks. Fold egg whites into batter.

Heat a pancake griddle and spray with cooking spray.

Scoop about 1/3 cup of batter onto the griddle for each cake and shape it into a round.

Cook about 4 to 5 minutes or until the edges are starting to dry. Then flip and cook for 1 to 2 minutes more.

Repeat with the remaining batter.

Serve.

Amaranth Oat Waffles

Preparation time: 15 minutes
Cooking time: 15 minutes
Servings: 14

Dry ingredients

Whole grain amaranth flour – 1 cup

Oat flour – ½ cup

Oat bran – ½ cup

Whole soy flour – ½ cup

Whole grain corn flour – ½ cup

Whole grain coarse cornmeal – ¼ cup

Flax meal – 2 Tbsp.

Baking powder – 2 ½ tsp.

Baking soda – ½ tsp.

Pinch sea salt

Wet ingredients

Equal parts of soy or almond milk – 2 ½ cups

Egg – 1 plus 2 egg whites

Unrefined sugar – ¼ cup

Vanilla extract – 1 tsp.

Cooking spray

Directions

Preheat waffle iron and grease it.

In a bowl, whisk the dry ingredients. In another bowl, whisk together the wet ingredients. Mix both wet and dry ingredients until just moistened.

Pour enough batter to cover cooking area. Close the lid.

Cook until waffle releases from iron.

Repeat with the remaining batter and serve.

Blueberry Baked Oatmeal

Preparation time: 10 minutes
Cooking time: 20 minutes
Servings: 5

Ingredients

Cooking spray

Unsweetened soy, rice, or almond milk – 1 cup

Whole egg – 1, plus 2 egg whites

Unsweetened applesauce – ½ cup

Pure maple syrup – 2 Tbsp.

Vanilla extract – ½ tsp.

Baking powder – 1 tsp.

Ground cinnamon – 1 tsp.

Freshly grated nutmeg – 1 pinch

Sea salt – 1 pinch

Old-fashioned rolled oats – 2 ½ cups

Oat bran – ¼ cup

Chopped pecans – ½ cup

Frozen or fresh blueberries – 1 ½ cups, divided

Directions

Preheat the oven to 350F.

Coat a 3-quart casserole dish with cooking spray.

Whisk together egg, egg whites, milk, applesauce, maple syrup, vanilla, baking powder, cinnamon, sea salt, and nutmeg.

Mix in oat bran, oats, and pecans.

Gently fold in half of the blueberries. Scatter remaining blueberries across the bottom of the casserole dish.

Scrape oatmeal mixture into a casserole dish and bake, uncovered, for 35 to 40 minutes, or until golden brown around the edges.

French Toast with Strawberries

Preparation time: 20 minutes
Cooking time: 5 to 7 minutes
Servings: 6

Ingredients

Firm tofu – 1 (12 oz.) package

Unsweetened soy, rice or almond milk – ½ cup

Pure maple syrup – 2 tsp.

Pure vanilla extract – 1 tsp.

Almond extract – ½ tsp.

Ground cinnamon – ½ tsp.

Pinch sea salt

Coconut oil – 2 Tbsp.

Whole grain bread – 6 slices

Sliced fresh strawberries – 1 ½ cups

Sliced almonds – 6 Tbsp.

Directions

To a blender, add the batter and blend until combined well. Pour into a bowl.

Heat a skillet

Then grease with oil.

Dip a slice of bread in batter, then turn it over and dip again to soak completely.

Place on the griddle and repeat until the griddle is covered with battered bread.

Sauté bread until the griddle is covered with battered bread.

Sauté bread until cooked through and browned, 2 to 3 minutes per side.

Top bread slices with sliced strawberries and almonds and serve.

Dark and Addictive Bran Muffins

Preparation time: 5 minutes
Cooking time: 20 minutes
Servings: 15

Ingredients

Cooking spray

Boiling water – 1 cup

Wheat bran – 1 cup

Wet ingredients

Coconut oil – 2 Tbsp. melted

Unrefined sugar – ¼ cup

Unsulfured blackstrap molasses

Unsweetened applesauce – ½ cup

Soy, rice or almond milk – 1 cup

Plain soy yogurt – 1 cup

Orange zest – 1 Tbsp.

Dry ingredients

Whole wheat flour – 2 ½ cups

Whole grain soy flour – 2 Tbsp.

Flax meal – 2 Tbsp.

Baking soda – 2 ½ tsp.

Sea salt – ¼ tsp.

All-natural, whole-grain bran flake cereal – 2 cups

Flaxseed for garnish

Directions

Keep the oven rack in the center.

Preheat to 400F.

Prepare a muffin tin by lining with cooking spray.

Pour boiling water over bran and set aside.

Whisk together wet ingredients until combined well.

In a bowl, whisk together dry ingredients until combined well. Add wet ingredients and mix. Add bran flake cereal and bran and water mixture, stir to combine.

Divide batter among 15 muffin cups and sprinkle the tops with flaxseeds.

Bake for 20 minutes.

Remove from the oven, cool and serve.

Brown Rice Breakfast

Preparation time: 5 minutes
Cooking time: 10 minutes
Servings: 2

Ingredients

Cooked brown rice – 2 cups

Unsweetened almond or soy milk – 2 cups

Sliced raw almonds – ¼ cup

Flaxseed – 1 Tbsp.

Maple syrup – 2 tsp. divided

Pinch of grated nutmeg

Directions

Divide rice between two bowls and add half of the milk and remaining ingredients to each.

Serve.

Smoothie on the Beach

Preparation time: 10 minutes
Cooking time: 0 minutes
Servings: 3

Ingredients

Soy yogurt – 2 cups

Frozen mango, pineapple chunks, strawberries, and peach slices

Hulled hem seeds – 1 Tbsp.

Golden flaxseed – 1 Tbsp.

Oat bran – 1 Tbsp.

Vegan protein powder – 2 Tbsp.

Pure vanilla extract – ½ tsp.

Juice of 1 lime

Directions

Place all ingredients in a blender

Blend until smooth.

Serve.

Buttermilk Bran Pancakes

Preparation time: 10 minutes
Cooking time: 10 minutes
Servings: 4

Ingredients

High-fiber wheat bran cereal – 1/3 cup

Buttermilk – 1 ¼ cup

Egg – 1

Brown sugar – 2 Tbsp. packed

Vegetable oil – 2 tsp.

All-purpose flour – 1 cup

Baking powder – 1 tsp.

Baking soda - -1/2 tsp.

Salt – ¼ tsp.

Chopped apple – ¼ cup

Coarsely chopped walnuts – ¼ cup

Sugar – 1 Tbsp.

Ground cinnamon – ¼ tsp.

Yogurt – 1/3 cup

Cooking spray and ground cinnamon

Directions

Place the cereal in a medium bowl. Add oil, brown sugar, egg, and buttermilk. Stir and mix well. Set aside for 10 minutes.

Meanwhile, in a small bowl, stir together baking soda, baking powder, flour, and salt. Sat aside.

For the topping: In another bowl, add walnuts and apple. Combine ¼ ts: cinnamon and sugar. Then toss with apple mixture. Stir yogurt to make it creamy. Then add on top of apple mixture.

Add flour mixture to the buttermilk mixture. Stir until combined.

Coat a pan with cooking spray.

Then heat on medium-low heat.

Pour ¼ cup of batter into the hot pan for each pancake. Cook until the bottom is golden, about 1 to 2 minutes, then flip and cook until golden, about 1 minute more.

Transfer to a serving plate.

Serve with apple-walnut topping and sprinkle with more cinnamon if desired.

Mexican Tomatillo-Poblano Eggs

Preparation time: 10 minutes
Cooking time: 5 minutes
Servings: 6

Ingredients

Fresh tomatillos – 2 pounds, husked and chopped

Fresh Poblano Chile peppers - 1 ½ cups (seeded and chopped)

Chopped onion – ½ cup

Fresh Serrano Chile pepper – 1 Tbsp. (seeded and finely chopped)

Garlic cloves – 2, minced

Ground cumin – 1 ½ tsp.

Dried oregano – 1 tsp. crushed

Salt – ½ tsp.

Ground coriander – ½ tsp.

Tortilla chips – ½ cup

Fresh cilantro – ¼ cup

Lime juice – 2 Tbsp.

Eggs – 6

Monterey Jack or Shredded Chihuahua Cheese – ¾ cup

Chili powder as needed

Directions

Combine first nine ingredients (through coriander) in a slow cooker.

Cook on high for 3 to 3 ½ minutes or low on 6 to 7 minute s.

Then turn the heat to high cooking on low.

Stir in cilantro, lime juice, and tortilla chips. Into a custard cup, break an egg and slip the egg into the tomato mixture. Repeat with the remaining eggs.

Cover and cook until eggs are cooked about 25 to 35 minutes.

Top servings with cilantro, chili powder, and cheese.

Serve with tortilla chips.

Vegetable Cheese Strata

Preparation time: Overnight

Cooking time: 25 minutes
Servings: 8

Ingredients

Nonstick cooking spray

Cubed Whole wheat French bread – 5 cups

Olive oil – 4 tsp.

Chopped onion – 1 cup

Chopped red sweet pepper – 1 cup

Garlic – 4 cloves, minced

Fresh Cremini Mushrooms – 2 cups, sliced

Lightly packed fresh spinach leaves – 3 cups

Shredded part-skim mozzarella cheese – 1 cup

Finely Shredded Parmesan cheese – 1/3 cup

Eggs – 8

Egg whites – 8

Fat-free milk – 1 ¾ cups

Dijon-style mustard – 1 Tbsp.

Salt – ½ tsp.

Black pepper – ½ tsp.

Directions

Lightly coat a baking dish (3-qt) with cooking spray. Then spread half of the bread cubes in it.

Heat 2 tsp. olive oil skillet. Add garlic, sweet pepper, onion and cook until tender. Stirring occasionally. Remove from skillet.

Add 2 tsp. oil to the skillet. Then add mushrooms. Cook and stir until tender. Add spinach and cook until slightly wilted. Stir in the onion mixture.

In a small bowl, mix both cheeses and reserve 1/3 cup.

Spread half of the vegetable mixture over bread cubes in the dish. Sprinkle with remaining cheese mixture. Layer with vegetable mixture and remaining bread cubes.

Whisk together the remaining ingredients in a large bowl. Then pour over the dish (on top of the mixture). Cover and chill overnight.

Preheat the oven to 325F. Bake, uncovered, for 45 minutes. Sprinkle with reserved 1/3 cup cheese mixture.

Bake for 5 to 10 minutes. Cool for 10 minutes before serving.

Creamy Fruit-Filled Crepes

Preparation time: 10 minutes
Cooking time: 10 minutes
Servings: 4

Ingredients

Egg – 1, lightly beaten

Fat-free milk – ¾ cup

All-purpose flour – ½ cup

Olive oil-1 Tbsp.

Salt – 1/8 tsp.

Desired topping

43

Directions

In a bowl, whisk together oil, salt, flour, milk, and egg until smooth.

Lightly grease a nonstick skillet and heat over medium heat.

Then remove the pan from the stove and add 2 Tbsp. batter. Tilt the batter to spread evenly.

Return to heat and cook until browned on the bottom, about 1 to 2 minutes. Remove and place on paper towels. Repeat with the remaining batter.

To assemble, place crepes on the serving plate (browned side down). Spoon desired filling onto half of each crepe, then fold.

Serve.

Breakfast Tacos

Preparation time: 10 minutes
Cooking time: 20 minutes
Servings: 4

Ingredients

Corn tortillas -6 inches

Vegetable oil – 1 tsp.

Salt – ¼ tsp.

Shredded hash brown potatoes – 1 cup, frozen

Chopped green sweet pepper – 2 Tbsp.

Eggs – 4, lightly beaten

Egg whites – 2

Salsa – 5 Tbsp.

Reduced sodium black beans – ½ cup, drained and rinsed

Shredded reduced-fat cheddar cheese – ¼ cup

Lime wedges and salsa

Directions

Place rack in the middle and preheat the oven to 375F.

Stack tortillas and wrap in damp paper towels. Microwave on high until softened and warm, about 40 seconds.

Brush both sides of the tortillas with oil and sprinkle with salt. Arrange the tortillas on the oven rack and bake until crisp, about 7 minutes. Transfer to a plate.

Meanwhile, coat a skillet with cooking spray and heat over medium heat.

Add sweet pepper and hash brown potatoes and cook until potatoes are light brown, about 2 to 3 minutes. Stirring occasionally.

In a small bowl, combine 1 Tbsp. salsa, egg whites, and eggs. Then pour the mixture over the potato mixture in the pan.

Cook, until the mixture starts to set, don't stir.

Then tilt the pan and/or lift the mixture with a spatula, so the uncooked portion gets cooked.

Continue to cook until the mixture is cooked completely, about 2 to 3 minutes more. Remove from the heat when cooked.

Add egg mixture into tortilla shells. Top with 4 Tbsp. salsa and beans. Sprinkle with cheese.

Serve with additional salsa and lime wedges.

Rice and Bean Frittata

Preparation time: 10 minutes
Cooking time: 20 minutes
Servings: 4

Ingredients

Vegetable oil – 2 Tbsp.

Sliced zucchini – 2 cups

Cooked long grain and wild rice – 1 (8.8 ounces) pouch

Garbanzo, or navy beans – 1 (15-ounce can), rinsed and drained

Eggs – 6, lightly beaten

Milk – ¼ cup

Salt – ¼ tsp.

Ground black pepper – ¼ tsp.

Shredded Colby and Monterey Jack Cheese – 1 cup

Cherry tomatoes or fresh parsley

Directions

Heat oil in a large skillet.

Add zucchini to the skillet. Cook and stir until crisp-tender.

Microwave rice according to package directions. Add the beans and rice in the skillet. Stir to combine.

In a bowl, combine milk, salt, pepper, and eggs. Then pour in the skillet over the rice mixture. Cook over medium heat.

Gently lift the edges to cook the mixture evenly. Cook until the mixture is set.

Sprinkle with cheese. Top with parsley and cherry tomatoes.

Serve.

Breakfast Pita Pizzas

Preparation time: 10 minutes
Cooking time: 20 minutes
Servings: 2

Ingredients

Olive oil – 1 tsp.

Sliced fresh mushrooms – ½ cup

Chopped red and green sweet pepper - ½ cup

Firm tub-style tofu – 3 ounces, drained and crumbled

Thinly sliced green onion – 2 Tbsp.

Garlic – 1 clove, minced

Ground black pepper – 1/8 tsp.

49

Whole wheat pita bread round – 1, split in half horizontally

Shredded reduced-fat cheddar cheese – ½ cup

Refrigerated fresh salsa – 1 cup

Directions

Preheat the oven to 375F.

Heat oil in a skillet.

Add sweet pepper and mushrooms and cook until tender, about 5 to 8 minutes. Stirring occasionally. Stir in black pepper, garlic, green onion, and tofu.

Place pita halves on a baking sheet cut sides down.

Sprinkle with ¼ cup of the cheese, then top with mushroom mixture. Then sprinkle with the rest of ¼-cup cheese.

Bake until heated through and cheese is melted about 8 to 10 minutes.

Cool, slice, and serve with salsa.

Waffle Sandwiches

Preparation time: 10 minutes
Cooking time: 10 minutes
Servings: 4

Ingredients

Light cream cheese – ½ cup, softened

Honey – 4 tsp.

Whole grain sandwich bread – 8 slices

Sliced fresh strawberries – 1 ½ cups

Low-fat granola – ¼ cup

Salted – 2 Tbsp. roasted sunflower kernels

Nonstick cooking spray and honey

Directions

Combine 4 tsp. honey and cream cheese in a small bowl. Spread cream cheese on one side of the bread slices.

Top four of the bread slices with sunflower kernels.

Then with granola, and strawberries.

Then top with the remaining four bread slices, spread sides down.

Coat a waffle baker with cooking spray and heat according to instructions.

One at a time, cook the sandwiches in the waffle bake until golden, about 2 minutes.

Remove with a fork when cooked.

Cut serve with additional honey.

Peanut Butter and Fruit Quinoa

Preparation time: 10 minutes
Cooking time: 15 minutes
Servings: 4

Ingredients

Water – 2 cups

Quinoa – 1 cup

Apple juice or cider – ¼ cup

Reduced-fat creamy peanut butter – 3 Tbsp.

Banana – 1 small, chopped

Raspberry or strawberry – 2 Tbsp.

Unsalted, blanched peanuts – 4 tsp.

Directions

Combine water and quinoa in a pan. Bring to a boil. Reduce heat to medium and cook until water is absorbed, about 10 to 15 minutes. Remove from heat. Add peanut butter and apple juice. Stir until combined. Stir in banana.

Divide mixture among bowls. Top each bowl with fruit and peanuts.

Serve.

Easy Huevos Rancheros

Preparation time: 10 minutes
Cooking time: 10 to 15 minutes
Servings: 1

Ingredients

Vegetable oil – 1 Tbsp.

Tortilla wrap – 1 corn

Egg – 1

Black beans – 200g can, drained

Juice of ½ lime

Ripe avocado – ½, peeled and sliced

Feta – 50g, crumbled

Hot chili sauce as needed

Directions

In a frying pan, heat oil over high heat.

Add the tortilla and fry until crisping at the edges, about 1 to 2 minutes on each side. Transfer to a plate.

Crack and add the eggs and cook as you like.

Meanwhile, tip the beans in a bowl. Add a squeeze of lime and season. Then lightly mash with a fork.

Spread the beans over the tortilla. Top with feta, avocado, egg and chili sauce.

Squeeze with a little juice and serve.

Oat Flour Pancakes

Preparation time: 10 minutes
Cooking time: 10 minutes
Servings: 5

Ingredients

Unsweetened applesauce – ½ cup

Oat flour rolled oats – 1 ¼ cup (ground in a blender)

Non-dairy milk – ½ cup

Lemon juice – 2 tsp.

Maple syrup – 2 Tbsp.

Baking powder – 1 tsp.

Baking soda – 1 tsp.

Vanilla extract – 1 tsp.

Directions

Combine everything in a blender.

Blend until combined, don't over blend.

Heat a non-stick skillet over medium heat.

Add 1/3 cup batter in the pan.

Then spread into a circle.

Cook for 2 to 3 minutes.

Then flip and cook another 2 to 3 minutes.

Repeat to finish.

Top with maple syrup, hemp seeds, and fruit.

Chapter 3: Salads and dressings

Artichoke and Green Olives with Walnut Vinaigrette

Preparation time: 10 minutes
Cooking time: 0 minutes
Servings: 5

Ingredients:

1 artichoke, rinsed & patted

½ cup green olives

Dressing

2 tbsp. red wine vinegar

4 tablespoons extra virgin olive oil

Freshly ground black pepper

3/4 cup finely coarsely ground walnuts

Sea salt

Combine all of the dressing ingredients in a food processor.

Toss with the rest of the ingredients and combine well.

Endive with Black Olives and Artichoke Hearts

Ingredients:

1 head Endive, rinsed, patted and shredded

½ cup black olives

½ cup artichoke hearts

Dressing

2 tbsp. apple cider vinegar

4 tablespoons olive oil

Freshly ground black pepper

3/4 cup finely ground almonds

Sea salt

Combine all of the dressing ingredients in a food processor.

Toss with the rest of the ingredients and combine well.

Swiss Chard and Artichoke Hearts with Black Olive Salad

Preparation time: 10 minutes
Cooking time: 0 minutes
Servings: 5

Ingredients:

1 head Swiss chard, rinsed, patted and shredded

½ cup black olives

½ cup artichoke hearts

Dressing

2 tbsp. white wine vinegar

4 tablespoons extra virgin olive oil

Freshly ground black pepper

3/4 cup finely ground peanuts

61

Sea salt

Combine all of the dressing ingredients in a food processor.

Toss with the rest of the ingredients and combine well.

Collard Greens Black Olive and Artichoke Heart Salad

Preparation time: 10 minutes
Cooking time: 0 minutes
Servings: 5

Ingredients:

1 bunch collard greens, rinsed, patted and shredded

½ cup black olives

½ cup artichoke hearts

Dressing

2 tbsp. red wine vinegar

4 tablespoons extra virgin olive oil

Freshly ground black pepper

3/4 cup finely ground almonds

Sea salt

Combine all of the dressing ingredients in a food processor.

Toss with the rest of the ingredients and combine well.

Heart with Macadamia Vinaigrette Salad

Preparation time: 10 minutes
Cooking time: 0 minutes
Servings: 5

Ingredients:

1 head romaine lettuce, rinsed, patted and shredded

½ cup black olives

½ cup artichoke hearts

Dressing

2 tbsp. balsamic vinegar

4 tablespoons macadamia oil

Freshly ground black pepper

3/4 cup finely coarsely ground cashews

Sea salt

Combine all of the dressing ingredients in a food processor.

Toss with the rest of the ingredients and combine well.

Bib Lettuce Black Olives and Artichoke Heart Salad

Preparation time: 10 minutes
Cooking time: 0 minutes
Servings: 5

Ingredients:

1 head bib lettuce, rinsed, patted and shredded

½ cup black olives

½ cup artichoke hearts

Dressing

2 tbsp. white wine vinegar

4 tablespoons extra virgin olive oil

Freshly ground black pepper

3/4 cup finely ground almonds

Sea salt

Combine all of the dressing ingredients in a food processor.

Toss with the rest of the ingredients and combine well.

Boston Lettuce with *Black* Olive Salad

Preparation time: 10 minutes
Cooking time: 0 minutes
Servings: 5

Ingredients:

1 head Boston lettuce, rinsed, patted and shredded

½ cup black olives

½ cup artichoke hearts

Dressing

2 tbsp. apple cider vinegar

4 tablespoons extra virgin olive oil

Freshly ground black pepper

3/4 cup finely ground peanuts

Sea salt

Combine all of the dressing ingredients in a food processor.

Toss with the rest of the ingredients and combine well.

Romaine Lettuce with Artichoke Heart and Cashew Vinaigrette Salad

Preparation time: 10 minutes
Cooking time: 0 minutes
Servings: 5

Ingredients:

1 head romaine lettuce, rinsed, patted and shredded

½ cup black olives

½ cup artichoke hearts

Dressing

2 tbsp. red wine vinegar

4 tablespoons olive oil

Freshly ground black pepper

3/4 cup finely coarsely ground cashews

71

Sea salt

Combine all of the dressing ingredients in a food processor.

Toss with the rest of the ingredients and combine well.

Mustard Greens Artichoke Heart and Green Olive Salad

Preparation time: 10 minutes
Cooking time: 0 minutes
Servings: 5

Ingredients:

1 bunch of mustard greens, rinsed, patted and shredded

½ cup green olives

½ cup artichoke hearts

Dressing

2 tbsp. red wine vinegar

4 tablespoons macadamia oil

Freshly ground black pepper

3/4 cup finely coarsely ground walnuts

Sea salt

Combine all of the dressing ingredients in a food processor.

Toss with the rest of the ingredients and combine well.

Beetroot Kalamata Olives and Artichoke Heart Salad

Preparation time: 10 minutes
Cooking time: 0 minutes
Servings: 5

Ingredients:

2 beetroots, peeled and sliced lengthwise

½ cup Kalamata olives

½ cup artichoke hearts

Dressing

2 tbsp. white wine vinegar

4 tablespoons extra virgin olive oil

Freshly ground black pepper

3/4 cup finely ground almonds

Sea salt

Combine all of the dressing ingredients in a food processor.

Toss with the rest of the ingredients and combine well.

Collard Greens Baby Corn and Artichoke Heart Salad

Preparation time: 10 minutes
Cooking time: 0 minutes
Servings: 5

Ingredients:

1 bunch of collard greens, rinsed, patted and shredded

½ cup baby corn

½ cup artichoke hearts

Dressing

2 tbsp. balsamic vinegar

4 tablespoons macadamia oil

Freshly ground black pepper

3/4 cup finely coarsely ground cashews

Sea salt

Combine all of the dressing ingredients in a food processor.

Toss with the rest of the ingredients and combine well.

Boston Lettuce Baby Carrots and Artichoke Heart Salad

Preparation time: 10 minutes
Cooking time: 0 minutes
Servings: 5

Ingredients:

1 head Boston lettuce, rinsed , patted and shredded

½ cup baby carrots

½ cup artichoke hearts

Dressing

2 tbsp. white wine vinegar

4 tablespoons extra virgin olive oil

Freshly ground black pepper

3/4 cup finely ground peanuts

Sea salt

Combine all of the dressing ingredients in a food processor.

Toss with the rest of the ingredients and combine well.

Kale Black Olives and Baby Corn Salad

Preparation time: 10 minutes
Cooking time: 0 minutes
Servings: 5

Ingredients:

1 bunch of kale, rinsed, patted and shredded

½ cup black olives

½ cup canned baby corn

Dressing

2 tbsp. apple cider vinegar

4 tablespoons olive oil

Freshly ground black pepper

3/4 cup finely ground almonds

Sea salt

Combine all of the dressing ingredients in a food processor.

Toss with the rest of the ingredients and combine well.

Romaine Lettuce & Baby Carrots with Walnut Vinaigrette Salad

Preparation time: 10 minutes
Cooking time: 0 minutes
Servings: 5

Ingredients:

1 bunch of kale, rinsed, patted and shredded

½ cup black olives

½ cup baby carrots

Dressing

2 tbsp. white wine vinegar

4 tablespoons extra virgin olive oil

Freshly ground black pepper

3/4 cup finely coarsely ground walnuts

Sea salt

Combine all of the dressing ingredients in a food processor.

Toss with the rest of the ingredients and combine well.

Boston Lettuce with Capers and Artichoke Heart Salad

Preparation time: 10 minutes
Cooking time: 0 minutes
Servings: 5

Ingredients:

1 bunch of mustard greens

½ cup capers

½ cup artichoke hearts

Dressing

2 tbsp. red wine vinegar

4 tablespoons extra virgin olive oil

Freshly ground black pepper

3/4 cup finely ground almonds

Sea salt

Combine all of the dressing ingredients in a food processor.

Toss with the rest of the ingredients and combine well.

Bib Lettuce Olive and Baby Carrot with Walnut Vinaigrette Salad

Preparation time: 10 minutes
Cooking time: 0 minutes
Servings: 5

Ingredients:

1 head bib lettuce, rinsed, patted and shredded

½ cup black olives

½ cup baby carrots

Dressing

2 tbsp. apple cider vinegar

4 tablespoons extra virgin olive oil

Freshly ground black pepper

3/4 cup finely coarsely ground walnuts

Sea salt

Combine all of the dressing ingredients in a food processor.

Toss with the rest of the ingredients and combine well.

Collard Greens with Baby Corn Salad

Preparation time: 15 minutes
Cooking time: 0 minutes
Servings: 5

Ingredients:

1 bunch of collard greens

½ cup black olives

½ cup canned baby corn

Dressing

2 tbsp. red wine vinegar

4 tablespoons extra virgin olive oil

Freshly ground black pepper

3/4 cup finely ground almonds

Sea salt

Combine all of the dressing ingredients in a food processor.

Toss with the rest of the ingredients and combine well.

Boston Lettuce Red Onion and Artichoke Heart with Peanut Vinaigrette Salad

Preparation time: 10 minutes
Cooking time: 0 minutes
Servings: 5

Ingredients:

1 head Boston lettuce, rinsed, patted and shredded

½ cup chopped red onion

½ cup artichoke hearts

5 ounces cream cheese, crumbled

Dressing

2 tbsp. white wine vinegar

4 tablespoons extra virgin olive oil

Freshly ground black pepper

3/4 cup finely ground peanuts

Sea salt

Combine all of the dressing ingredients in a food processor.

Toss with the rest of the ingredients and combine well.

Bib Lettuce Black Olives and Baby Corn with Almond Vinaigrette Salad

Preparation time: 10 minutes
Cooking time: 0 minutes
Servings: 5

Ingredients:

1 head Bib lettuce, rinsed, patted and shredded

½ cup black olives

½ cup canned baby corn

Dressing

2 tbsp. white wine vinegar

4 tablespoons olive oil

Freshly ground black pepper

3/4 cup finely ground almonds

Sea salt

Combine all of the dressing ingredients in a food processor.

Toss with the rest of the ingredients and combine well.

Endive and Green Olive Salad

Preparation time: 10 minutes
Cooking time: 0 minutes
Servings: 5

Ingredients:

1 endives rinsed, patted and shredded

½ cup green olives

½ cup artichoke hearts

Dressing

2 tbsp. white wine vinegar

4 tablespoons macadamia oil

Freshly ground black pepper

3/4 cup finely coarsely ground cashews

Sea salt

Combine all of the dressing ingredients in a food processor.

Toss with the rest of the ingredients and combine well.

Mixed Greens Olives and Artichoke Heart Salad

Preparation time: 10 minutes
Cooking time: 0 minutes
Servings: 5

Ingredients:

1 bunch of mixed greens, rinsed, patted and shredded

½ cup black olives

½ cup artichoke hearts

Dressing

2 tbsp. white wine vinegar

4 tablespoons extra virgin olive oil

Freshly ground black pepper

3/4 cup finely coarsely ground walnuts

Sea salt

Combine all of the dressing ingredients in a food processor.

Toss with the rest of the ingredients and combine well.

Iceberg Lettuce and Artichoke Heart Salad

Preparation time: 10 minutes
Cooking time: 0 minutes
Servings: 5

Ingredients:

1 head Iceberg lettuce, rinsed, patted and shredded

½ cup Kalamata olives

½ cup artichoke hearts

5 ounces ricotta cheese

Dressing

2 tbsp. balsamic vinegar

4 tablespoons extra virgin olive oil

Freshly ground black pepper

3/4 cup finely ground almonds

Sea salt

Combine all of the dressing ingredients in a food processor.

Toss with the rest of the ingredients and combine well.

Artichoke Capers and Artichoke Heart Salad

Preparation time: 10 minutes
Cooking time: 0 minutes
Servings: 5

Ingredients:

1 artichoke, rinsed, patted and shredded

½ cup capers

½ cup artichoke hearts

Dressing

2 tbsp. white wine vinegar

4 tablespoons extra virgin olive oil

Freshly ground black pepper

3/4 cup finely ground almonds

Sea salt

Combine all of the dressing ingredients in a food processor.

Toss with the rest of the ingredients and combine well.

Mixed Greens Baby Corn and Artichoke Heart Salad

Preparation time: 10 minutes
Cooking time: 0 minutes
Servings: 5

Ingredients:

1 bunch Mesclun, rinsed, patted and shredded

½ cup canned baby corn

½ cup artichoke hearts

Dressing

2 tbsp. white wine vinegar

4 tablespoons extra virgin olive oil

Freshly ground black pepper

3/4 cup finely ground peanuts

Sea salt

Combine all of the dressing ingredients in a food processor.

Toss with the rest of the ingredients and combine well.

Bib Lettuce with Tomatillo Dressing

Preparation time: 10 minutes
Cooking time: 0 minutes
Servings: 5

Ingredients:

1 head Bib lettuce, shredded

4 large tomatoes, seeded and chopped

4 radishes, thinly sliced

Dressing

6 tomatillos, rinsed and halved

1 jalapeno, halved

1 white onion, quartered

2 tablespoons extra virgin olive oil

Kosher salt and freshly ground black pepper

1/2 teaspoon ground cumin

1 cup Dairy free cream cheese

2 tablespoons fresh lemon juice

Preheat the oven to 400 degrees F.

For the dressing, place the tomatillos, jalapeno and onion on a cookie sheet.

Drizzle with olive oil and sprinkle with salt and pepper.

Roast in the oven for 25-30 min. until vegetables begin to brown and slightly darken.

Transfer to a food processor and let it cool then blend.

Add the rest of the ingredients and refrigerate for an minute .

Toss with the rest of the ingredients and combine well.

Enoki Mushroom and Cucumber Salad

Preparation time: 10 minutes
Cooking time: 0 minutes
Servings: 5

Ingredients:

15 Enoki Mushrooms, thinly sliced

1/4 white onion, peeled, halved lengthwise, and thinly sliced

1 large cucumber, halved lengthwise and thinly sliced

Dressing

¼ cup extra-virgin olive oil

2 splashes white wine vinegar

Coarse salt and black pepper

Combine all of the dressing ingredients.

Toss with the rest of the ingredients and combine well.

Tomato and Zucchini Salad

Preparation time: 10 minutes
Cooking time: 0 minutes
Servings: 5

Ingredients:

1/4 white onion, peeled, halved lengthwise, and thinly sliced

1 large Zucchini halved lengthwise ,thinly sliced & blanched

5 ounces mozarella cheese, shredded

Dressing

¼ cup extra-virgin olive oil

2 tbsp. apple cider vinegar

Coarse salt and black pepper

Combine all of the dressing ingredients.

Toss with the rest of the ingredients and combine well.

Tomatillos with Cucumber and Ricotta Cheese Salad

Ingredients:

10 Tomatillos, halved lengthwise, seeded, and thinly sliced

1/4 white onion, peeled, halved lengthwise, and thinly sliced

1 large cucumber, halved lengthwise and thinly sliced

5 ounces ricotta cheese

Dressing

¼ cup extra-virgin olive oil

2 splashes white wine vinegar

Coarse salt and black pepper

Combine all of the dressing ingredients.

Toss with the rest of the ingredients and combine well.

Plum Tomato and Onion Salad

Preparation time: 10 minutes
Cooking time: 0 minutes
Servings: 5

Ingredients:

1/4 white onion, peeled, halved lengthwise, and thinly sliced

1 large cucumber, halved lengthwise and thinly sliced

Dressing

¼ cup extra-virgin olive oil

2 tbsp. apple cider vinegar

Coarse salt and black pepper

Prep

Combine all of the dressing ingredients.

Toss with the rest of the ingredients and combine well.

Zucchini Pepperjack Cheese and Tomato Salad

Preparation time: 20 minutes
Cooking time: 0 minutes
Servings: 5

Ingredients:

1/4 white onion, peeled, halved lengthwise, and thinly sliced

1 large Zucchini halved lengthwise ,thinly sliced and blanched

5 ounces pepperjack cheese, shredded

Dressing

¼ cup extra-virgin olive oil

2 splashes white wine vinegar

Coarse salt and black pepper

Combine all of the dressing ingredients.

Toss with the rest of the ingredients and combine well.

Heirloom Tomato Salad

Preparation time: 20 minutes
Cooking time: 0 minutes
Servings: 5

Ingredients:

3 Heirloom tomatoes, halved lengthwise, seeded, and thinly sliced

1/4 white onion, peeled, halved lengthwise, and thinly sliced

1 large cucumber, halved lengthwise and thinly sliced

Dressing

¼ cup extra-virgin olive oil

2 splashes white wine vinegar

Coarse salt and black pepper

Combine all of the dressing ingredients.

Toss with the rest of the ingredients and combine well.

Enoki Mushroom and Feta Cheese Salad

Preparation time: 20 minutes
Cooking time: 0 minutes
Servings: 5

Ingredients:

15 Enoki Mushrooms, thinly sliced

1/4 white onion, peeled, halved lengthwise, and thinly sliced

1 large cucumber, halved lengthwise and thinly sliced

5 ounces feta cheese, crumbled

Dressing

¼ cup extra-virgin olive oil

2 tbsp. apple cider vinegar

Coarse salt and black pepper

Combine all of the dressing ingredients.

Toss with the rest of the ingredients and combine well.

Artichoke Heart and Plum Tomato Salad

Preparation time: 20 minutes
Cooking time: 0 minutes
Servings: 5

Ingredients:

6 Artichoke Hearts (Canned)

1/4 white onion, peeled, halved lengthwise, and thinly sliced

1 large cucumber, halved lengthwise and thinly sliced

Dressing

¼ cup extra-virgin olive oil

2 splashes white wine vinegar

Coarse salt and black pepper

Combine all of the dressing ingredients.

Toss with the rest of the ingredients and combine well.

Artichoke Heart and Plum Tomato Salad

Preparation time: 20 minutes
Cooking time: 0 minutes
Servings: 5

Ingredients:

6 Artichoke Hearts (Canned)

1/4 white onion, peeled, halved lengthwise, and thinly sliced

1 large cucumber, halved lengthwise and thinly sliced

Dressing

¼ cup extra-virgin olive oil

2 splashes white wine vinegar

Coarse salt and black pepper

Combine all of the dressing ingredients.

Toss with the rest of the ingredients and combine well.

Baby Corn and Plum Tomato Salad

Preparation time: 20 minutes
Cooking time: 0 minutes
Servings: 5

Ingredients:

½ cup canned baby corn

1/4 white onion, peeled, halved lengthwise, and thinly sliced

1 large Zucchini halved lengthwise ,thinly sliced and blanched

5 ounces cream cheese, crumbled

106

Dressing

¼ cup extra-virgin olive oil

2 splashes white wine vinegar

Coarse salt and black pepper

Combine all of the dressing ingredients.

Toss with the rest of the ingredients and combine well.

Mixed Greens Feta Cheese and Tomato Salad

Preparation time: 15 minutes
Cooking time: 0 minutes
Servings: 4

Ingredients:

1 bunch Meslcun, rinsed and drained

1/4 white onion, peeled, halved lengthwise, and thinly sliced

1 large cucumber, halved lengthwise and thinly sliced

5 ounces feta cheese, crumbled

Dressing

¼ cup extra-virgin olive oil

2 tbsp. apple cider vinegar

Coarse salt and black pepper

Combine all of the dressing ingredients.

Toss with the rest of the ingredients and combine well.

Artichoke and Tomato Salad

Preparation time: 15 minutes
Cooking time: 0 minutes
Servings: 4

Ingredients:

1 Artichoke, rinsed and drained

1/4 white onion, peeled, halved lengthwise, and thinly sliced

1 large Zucchini halved lengthwise ,thinly sliced and blanched

Dressing

¼ cup extra-virgin olive oil

2 splashes white wine vinegar

Coarse salt and black pepper

Combine all of the dressing ingredients.

Toss with the rest of the ingredients and combine well.

Spinach and Heirloom Tomato Salad

Preparation time: 15 minutes
Cooking time: 0 minutes
Servings: 4

Ingredients:

1 bunch Spinach, rinsed and drained

3 Heirloom tomatoes, halved lengthwise, seeded, and thinly sliced

1/4 white onion, peeled, halved lengthwise, and thinly sliced

1 large cucumber, halved lengthwise and thinly sliced

Dressing

¼ cup extra-virgin olive oil

2 tbsp. apple cider vinegar

Coarse salt and black pepper

Combine all of the dressing ingredients.

Toss with the rest of the ingredients and combine well.

Mesclun and Tomatillo Salad

Preparation time: 15 minutes
Cooking time: 0 minutes
Servings: 4

Ingredients:

1 bunch Mesclun, rinsed and drained

10 Tomatillos, halved lengthwise, seeded, and thinly sliced

1/4 white onion, peeled, halved lengthwise, and thinly sliced

1 large cucumber, halved lengthwise and thinly sliced

5 ounces cottage cheese

Dressing

¼ cup extra-virgin olive oil

2 splashes white wine vinegar

Coarse salt and black pepper

Combine all of the dressing ingredients.

Toss with the rest of the ingredients and combine well.

Mesclun and Enoki Mushroom Salad

Preparation time: 15 minutes
Cooking time: 0 minutes
Servings: 4

Ingredients:

1 bunch Meslcun, rinsed and drained

15 Enoki Mushrooms, thinly sliced

1/4 white onion, peeled, halved lengthwise, and thinly sliced

1 large cucumber, halved lengthwise and thinly sliced

5 ounces ricotta cheese

Dressing

¼ cup extra-virgin olive oil

2 splashes white wine vinegar

Coarse salt and black pepper

Combine all of the dressing ingredients.

Toss with the rest of the ingredients and combine well.

Bib Lettuce and Cucumber Salad

Preparation time: 15 minutes
Cooking time: 0 minutes
Servings: 4

Ingredients:

1 bunch Bib Lettuce, rinsed and drained

1/4 white onion, peeled, halved lengthwise, and thinly sliced

1 large cucumber, halved lengthwise and thinly sliced

Dressing

¼ cup extra-virgin olive oil

2 tbsp. apple cider vinegar

Coarse salt and black pepper

Combine all of the dressing ingredients.

Toss with the rest of the ingredients and combine well.

Kale Spinach and Zucchini with Cream Cheese Salad

Preparation time: 15 minutes
Cooking time: 0 minutes
Servings: 4

Ingredients:

1 bunch Kale, rinsed and drained

1 bunch Spinach, rinsed and drained

1/4 white onion, peeled, halved lengthwise, and thinly sliced

1 large Zucchini halved lengthwise ,thinly sliced and blanched

5 ounces cream cheese

Dressing

¼ cup extra-virgin olive oil

2 splashes white wine vinegar

Coarse salt and black pepper

Combine all of the dressing ingredients.

Toss with the rest of the ingredients and combine well.

Artichoke Spinach and Enoki Mushroom Salad

Preparation time: 15 minutes
Cooking time: 0 minutes
Servings: 4

Ingredients:

1 Artichoke, rinsed and drained

1 bunch Spinach, rinsed and drained

15 Enoki Mushrooms, thinly sliced

1/4 white onion, peeled, halved lengthwise, and thinly sliced

1 large cucumber, halved lengthwise and thinly sliced

5 ounces feta cheese, crumbled

Dressing

¼ cup extra-virgin olive oil

2 splashes white wine vinegar

Coarse salt and black pepper

Combine all of the dressing ingredients.

Toss with the rest of the ingredients and combine well.

Kale and Artichoke Salad

Preparation time: 15 minutes
Cooking time: 0 minutes
Servings: 4

Ingredients:

1 bunch Kale, rinsed and drained

1 Artichoke, rinsed and drained

1 large cucumber, halved lengthwise and thinly sliced

5 ounces mozarella cheese, shredded

Dressing

¼ cup extra-virgin olive oil

2 splashes white wine vinegar

Coarse salt and black pepper

Combine all of the dressing ingredients.

Toss with the rest of the ingredients and combine well.

Conclusion

The book has been written for those people who are not only health conscious, but also for those people who want to prepare exciting vegetarian dishes. Veggies are not only full of roughage and fibers, but also help in maintaining a complete balanced diet. The ingredients in the eBook are written perfectly with the tips and their actual quantity. The best thing about the eBook is that I have made sure that I have used the most cheaply available products in the market. Each and every ingredient can be gathered from the market, and I have also shown my different experiment with texture and taste. In the book we also find that vegetarian dishes not only include the main courses, but also deserts and sweets. The dishes give you a fine dining experience and even make you have a healthy diet control.

The path to a healthy body and mind is paved with fresh, wholesome, and real food. Everyone knows that eating more vegetables and grains are good for them. However, for beginners, this can be difficult because easy to make, and prep recipes are hand to find. This cookbook offers 50 approachable and delicious meatless recipes.

Go into this with a full force and reap all the benefits that come with it. Your mind will be in the zone and you will enjoy a healthier lifestyle. Keep in mind that you are not saying "no" to anything, but simply finding ways to enjoy the things that you love without the things that are detrimental to your health.

Wishing you a happy and healthy vegetarian lifestyle!